Christianit

A brief description of tl Church

Geoffrey Turner

Edward Arnold

Foreword

It has long been assumed that Christianity is adequately covered in the classroom by studying the New Testament and stopping, chronologically, around the end of the first century. It has also usually been assumed that pupils have an adequate working knowledge of the present-day Church. Neither assumption is justified. This book attempts to cover some of the missing ground, but in a very basic and, I hope, uncomplicated way. Some teachers may think that in doing so some important points have been oversimplified, but the teacher can always correct this by adding extra material of his own. The book looks at Christianity today and uses history only to the extent that it is necessary to supply an historical perspective for understanding twentieth-century Christianity. *Christianity* is unavoidably highly selective: many groups, such as the Orthodox Churches, the Brethren and Christian Scientists, have been omitted apart from a passing mention. If any such groups are represented in the classroom the teacher must deal with them as he thinks appropriate.

I believe very strongly that a textbook such as this must be given life, not only by discussions but by (judiciously chosen) visiting speakers, visits, slides and films. Some suggestions for films have been made but I must admit that I have not been able to watch all of these. The questions supplied after each chapter are only suggestions and the teacher may use them, add to them, or replace them as he or she wishes.

I would like to thank Mary Bevan, Bill Smith and Gordon Smith of Kingswood School, Corby, for helping with some of the initial preparation of this work and for trying it out in the classroom.

G. T.

Contents

1	How Christianity Came to Britain	5
2	The Reformation—the Origin of Christian Divisions	11
3	What Christians Believe	19
4	The Roman Catholic Church	29
5	The Church of England	39
6	The Methodist Church	49
7	The Nonconformist Churches	54
8	The World Council of Churches	60
9	The Church Abroad	64
10	What Christians Do	68
11	How Christians Worship	74
12	The Future of Christianity	78

Acknowledgements

The Publisher's thanks are due to the following for permission to reproduce copyright photographs: Religious Society of Friends, p. 4 (*centre,* Richard Haynes); Catholic Herald, p. 4 (*bottom right,* J. Higham); Leigh-on-Mendip Church, p. 4 (*bottom left,* Rev. John Fisher); The Methodist Recorder, p. 4 (*top left*: F. D. Wilson, *top right*); Popperfoto, pp. 7, 69, 75; Radio Times Hulton Picture Library, pp. 8, 12, 16, 48, 57; The Mansell Collection, pp. 13, 15, 18, 22, 26, 40; Keystone Press Agency, pp. 31, 37, 70; Noeline Kelly, pp. 35, 79; Church Information Office, p. 44; United Society for the Propagation of the Gospel, pp. 46, 65, 67; Methodist Home Mission, p. 52; Bournemouth News and Picture Service, p. 55; Rex Features, p. 58; World Council of Churches, pp. 61 (John Taylor), 62, 63; Camera Press, p. 66 (Baron); The Salvation Army, p. 71; Cinema International Corporation, p. 77; United Press, p. 32.

1

How Christianity Came to Britain

Look around. How many Christian churches are there in your town? Perhaps there is a cathedral or some other medieval church. Besides Church of England buildings, how many Roman Catholic churches are there? How many Methodist or other Protestant churches? Is there a meeting house belonging to the Society of Friends, or a hall for the Salvation Army? How did all these groups get here? When did they start? What do they believe and what do they do?

The history of the Christian Church has its origin in the life of Jesus, son of Joseph, the carpenter from Nazareth in Palestine, in the early part of the first century. It is to him that we must trace the origin of Christianity.

The first followers of Jesus of Nazareth were Jews who believed that Jesus was the Messiah that God had sent to free the Jews from their oppressors. Most of the Jewish people, however, would not accept Jesus as the Messiah. Immediately after Jesus had died his followers preached the message of freedom through Jesus Christ only to the Jews, but after a few years it was decided that they should also preach their good news to the Gentiles, those who were not Jews. *Paul* was the first to do this and he went on a series of missionary journeys in Asia Minor and even as far as Rome, trying to persuade Gentiles and Jews living abroad to become followers of Christ. It was soon after this that the Jews forced the Christians out of the Jewish synagogues and Christianity reluctantly became a separate religion.

Christianity rapidly spread among the lower classes and slaves of the Roman Empire, but Christians were frequently persecuted and killed by the Romans. This changed in AD 312 when the Roman Emperor, *Constantine*, freely allowed his citizens to become Christians. It soon became the favoured religion of the Empire and Constantine was himself baptised on his death-bed.

How Christianity Came to Britain

SCOTLAND
Iona
Aidan 634
Lindisfarne
Columbia 563
IRELAND
York
Patrick 432
WALES
Paulinus 627
ENGLAND
London
Canterbury
Augustine 597

Christianity had been gradually introduced into Britain during the time that it was occupied by the Romans. The first Briton to die for his Christian beliefs was *St Alban* who was killed about AD 250. When Britain was invaded nearly 200 years later by the Angles and Saxons from north Europe, the Christian Britons retreated into Wales and Cornwall and England became a pagan country. The Angles and Saxons introduced their own gods, among them Woden and Thor whose names are remembered in the days of the week, Wednesday and Thursday. It is thought that King Arthur was a Christian chieftain who fought successfully against the Saxons.

Christianity moved from Wales to Ireland when *St Patrick*, a Briton who was also a Roman citizen, sailed in AD 432 to convert the Irish. Approximately 100 years later in AD 563, *St Columba* took Christianity to the Western Isles of Scotland and established a monastic community on the island of Iona. In 634 *St Aidan* took the gospel to the rest of Scotland and the north of England. Aidan founded a monastery on the small island of Lindisfarne (now known as Holy Island) off the coast of Northumberland. Christianity had now moved in a circle from southern England to northern England by way of Wales, Ireland and Scotland.

St Augustine, from an early manuscript

How Christianity Came to Britain

Meanwhile, a small group of Benedictine monks had been sent from Rome by Pope Gregory to preach to the Saxons of Kent and the south of England. *St Augustine*, with his companions, landed in Kent in AD 597 and founded his first church in Canterbury. He became the first Bishop of Canterbury and this is why the Archbishop of Canterbury is still the chief bishop of the Church of England. One of Augustine's companions, St Paulinus, travelled north and became the first Bishop of York in AD 627.

The Celtic monks in the north had slightly different customs from the Roman monks in the south, even though they shared the same basic beliefs about Christianity; for example, they held their services in rather different ways and they laid less emphasis on the importance of the Bishop of Rome as the chief bishop of the Christian world. It was, among other things, a quarrel about this last point that became important at the time of the Reformation. But in the seventh century most of the differences were reconciled at a meeting of church leaders at the Abbey of Whitby in 663.

Most of this information about the coming of Christianity to Britain has been passed on to us in the *History of the English Church and People* which was written in 731 by *Bede*, a monk who lived and worked in Jarrow. Bede never travelled further than Lindisfarne and York yet he was known as an historian throughout Europe and he represents the scholarship of the English monks at its finest. From this time Britain was completely Christian and accepted until the Reformation—though sometimes grudgingly—that the Pope, that is the Bishop of Rome, was the Head of the Church.

1 The opposition that the early Christians met from Jews who rejected Jesus can be seen by reading *Acts*, Ch. 5, vv. 12–42 and Ch. 7, v. 54–Ch. 8, v. 3.
2 Paul was a Jew who, under the name of Saul, was a vigorous persecutor of these Christians. However, he had an extraordinary experience which changed him completely. Read about this in *Acts*, Ch. 9, vv. 1–31.
3 Read about the hardships that Paul had to undergo in preaching the gospel of Jesus Christ in *2 Corinthians*, Ch. 11, vv. 24–33.
4 From your library try to discover something about the life and work of the Iona Community on the island of Iona now.

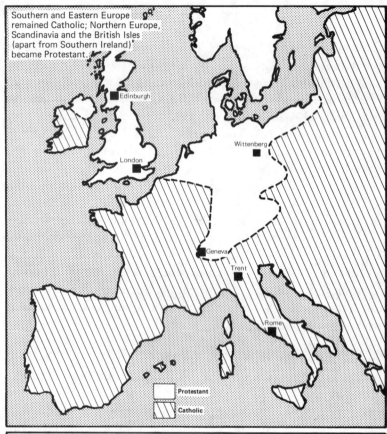

Southern and Eastern Europe remained Catholic; Northern Europe, Scandinavia and the British Isles (apart from Southern Ireland) became Protestant.

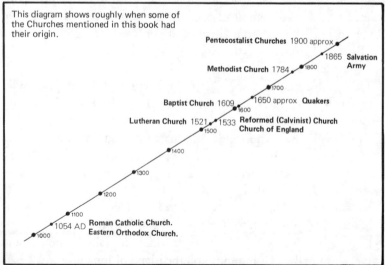

This diagram shows roughly when some of the Churches mentioned in this book had their origin.

Pentecostalist Churches 1900 approx
1865 Salvation Army
Methodist Church 1784
1650 approx Quakers
Baptist Church 1609
Lutheran Church 1521 1533 Reformed (Calvinist) Church
Church of England
1054 AD Roman Catholic Church.
Eastern Orthodox Church.

2

The Reformation—the Origin of Christian Divisions

The divisions between the different Christian denominations today can be traced back to their historical source—the Reformation. This, in fact, was not the first major split in the Church because the Eastern Orthodox Churches separated from the Roman Catholic Church in 1054. The split followed after a dispute over a technical detail in belief about the Holy Spirit, but in fact it had more to do with the fact that the Orthodox Christians considered that the Pope and his representatives behaved in an arrogant and high-handed way in Church matters. Today the Orthodox Churches preserve their distinctive customs, mainly in Eastern Europe.

The *Reformation* was a popular movement in northern Europe at the beginning of the sixteenth century which tried to simplify Christian belief, to insist on the importance of the Bible and to remove the moral laxity which had become quite common among the Catholic priesthood. The man who had most impact on this reform movement was a young monk and priest called *Martin Luther*. Luther became a lecturer on scripture at the University of Wittenberg, now in East Germany, and he had a spiritual conversion after having studied what Paul said about faith in his Letter to the Romans. The story is that Luther nailed to the door of Wittenberg Cathedral in 1517 a list of 95 theses; these theses were statements about the teaching of the Church which were intended for public debate. It is probably a legend that Luther actually nailed up the paper, but he did find himself involved in a series of debates with Johann Eck, with Cardinal Cajetan, and with the greatest of Catholic scholars at that time, *Erasmus* of Rotterdam. As a result of Luther's refusal to submit to the decisions of the Pope in these debates, he was finally *excommunicated* (that is, excluded from the Christian community) in 1521. 1521, then, marks the true beginning of the Reformation,

Martin Luther (1483–1546)

because from this time Luther and his followers had to form their own Church. This was the origin of the Lutheran Church which is still the main Protestant Church in Germany and Scandinavia. There are also many Lutherans in the United States but relatively few in Britain.

All those who followed Luther in his rebellion against the Catholic Church were known as *Protestants*. They acquired this name because they protested against some of the beliefs and behaviour of the Popes and Catholic clergy. But, more importantly, they were proud to be called Protestants because it indicated that they professed belief in the Bible, the Word of God, which they thought had been neglected by the Catholic Church.

The other major centre of the Reformation on the continent, apart

John Calvin (1509–1564)

from Wittenberg, was Geneva in Switzerland. It was here that *John Calvin* enforced a strict religious discipline after he had been appointed leader of the Church there in 1541. Calvin was the greatest theologian among the Reformers, and *The Institutes of the Christian Religion* is his most important book. He was the leader of the Protestant movement in Switzerland and France. At about this time Calvin was visited by a Scotsman, *John Knox*, who described Geneva as 'the most perfect school of Christ since the days of the Apostles'. Having been inspired by life in Geneva, Knox travelled to Scotland and became the leading light of the Church of Scotland which still follows the tradition of Calvin and Knox.

The Reformation in England was dominated by politics to a much greater extent than elsewhere. Henry VIII was a Catholic and a supporter of the Pope against Luther, but in 1527 he announced that he wanted to divorce his wife Catherine to whom he had been married for 17 years. As a previous Pope had already given Henry special permission to marry Catherine in the first place, the present Pope, Clement VII, did not feel that he could now give Henry permission to leave her. The two sides were deadlocked and the only way Henry could get his divorce, so that he could marry again and produce a son to succeed him as king, was to separate the Church in England from the authority of the Bishop of Rome. Henry found widespread support for this and those who were less than enthusiastic were executed if they publicly refused to accept Henry as Head of the Church of England. Most people accepted this, but a few did refuse and these included Thomas More and Bishop John Fisher, who were beheaded. The leader of the religious movement in England against Rome was *Thomas Cranmer* who was eventually made Archbishop of Canterbury.

After the short reign of Edward VI, there was a brief period when England returned to the Catholic form of Christianity under Mary Tudor. When Elizabeth Tudor became Queen in 1558 she ensured that the Church of England returned to a form of Protestantism, but not such an extreme form as that of the Lutheran Church or the Church of Scotland, for example. And from that time the Church of England has been the official Church in England.

A number of other Protestant groups appeared in England during the reign of Elizabeth I. These Churches were made up of Christians who thought that the Church of England had not gone far enough in reforming Christianity. They wanted a return to the Church of the first century as it is described in the New Testament. The *Congregationalists*, for example, thought that each congregation should be self-governing, without the need for bishops. The *Presbyterians* objected to the leaders of each congregation being called 'priests'; they preferred the New Testament word 'presbyter' (the Greek *presbuteros* means 'elder'). Similarly, the *Baptists* objected to the baptism of babies as this was not done in the New Testament, and the *Puritans* opposed any form of worship which could not be found in the New Testament. The Bible was the touchstone, the final

Henry VIII, born 1491, reigned 1509–47, in a portrait by Holbein. An accomplished musician, poet and author, Henry made himself the first Head of the Church of England.

authority, for the beliefs of all these groups. The early Protestants, however, did not find life easy in the reign of Elizabeth (as we shall see later) because for political reasons she wanted all Englishmen and women to share the same religion, the religion of the Church of England.

Erasmus of Rotterdam (1469–1536), by Holbein (detail)

The Reformation was a protest movement against moral corruption and against some of the beliefs of Catholicism, but it should not be thought that all Roman Catholics were lax and unprincipled. Many people who remained Catholic, like Erasmus, were appalled by the behaviour of some of the clergy, but they did not feel able to abandon their Church and form a new organisation. They could not accept the new ideas of the Reformers, but they did eventually start an attempt to reform the Catholic Church from the inside. A Council of Catholic bishops met periodically at Trent in north Italy between 1545 and 1563 in order to correct abuses in their Church and to re-express their beliefs about Christianity. This movement was known as the Counter-Reformation and its best-known member was *St Ignatius Loyola*, a Spaniard who formed the Society of Jesus, a religious order of priests popularly known as the *Jesuits*.

The Reformation—the Origin of Christian Divisions

If the Reformers had been less provocative and if successive Popes and other Catholics had been more tactful, the Christian Church might perhaps have been reformed without the widespread disruption that actually occurred. It is because the present divisions within the Christian Church were caused largely by disputes which are more than 400 years old that Christians think it is now possible to change the course of history. Catholics and Protestants now feel able to talk to each other and to co-operate with each other in a way which makes it possible that at some time in the future the divisions of the past may be overcome.

1. Luther rediscovered the Bible by reading Paul on 'faith'. Read *Romans*, Ch. 5, vv. 1–11 carefully (twice) and explain why, according to Paul, Jesus Christ is important. Read also *Romans*, Ch. 7, v. 24–Ch. 8, v. 11. How are Christians changed by the Spirit of God?
2. To discover more about the life of Luther, obtain from your library a copy of *Here I Stand: A Life of Martin Luther* by Roland Bainton. Find out what happened at Rome in 1510, at Wittenberg in 1517, the Wartburg in 1521 and Eisleben in 1546. What did Luther say at Worms in April 1521? What did Luther produce in September 1522?
3. Luther's life has been dramatised in the play *Luther* by John Osborne. This is not suitable for play reading, as it contains many long speeches, but you could try reading individually Act Two, Scene Three, set in Wittenberg, and Act Three, Scene One, set in Worms.
4. The trial of Thomas More has been dramatised in *A Man For All Seasons* by Robert Bolt (and a film has been made of it). This is suitable for acting or play reading. If you do not want to go through it all, try the scene where Henry VIII visits the home of Thomas More to discuss the possibility of his divorce from Catherine of Aragon, and the trial scene at the end when More is found guilty of treason for not accepting Henry as Head of the Church of England.
5. A film called *Erasmus* (16 mins, black and white) is available from Concord Films Council Ltd., Nacton, Ipswich, Suffolk.

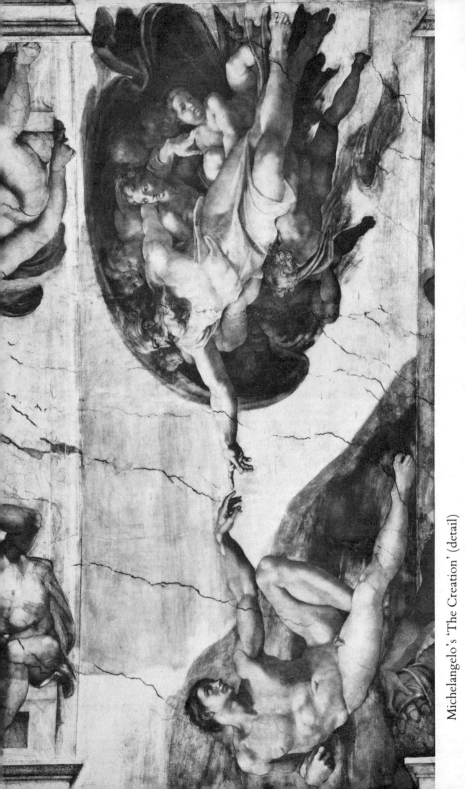

Michelangelo's 'The Creation' (detail)

3

What Christians Believe

The Christian Church divided into a number of separate denominations at the Reformation, yet the basic beliefs of Christianity are shared by all Christians, although they are sometimes understood in slightly different ways. From the earliest times Christians have expressed these basic beliefs in *creeds*. The word 'creed' comes from the Latin *credo*, which means 'I believe', the first words of a creed. Here is the Apostles' Creed which was traditionally thought to have been written by the Apostles. This is not true but we do know that this creed was used from the fourth century in Rome and was recited at the baptism of adults. It is a slightly shorter and simpler version of the creed which is still recited in the services of the Church of England, and less frequently in other Churches.

> I believe in God almighty,
> And in Jesus Christ, his only son, our Lord,
> Who was born of the Holy Spirit and the Virgin Mary,
> Who was crucified under Pontius Pilate and was buried,
> And on the third day rose from the dead;
> He ascended into heaven
> And sits at the right hand of the Father,
> From where he will come to judge the living and the dead.
> And I believe in the Holy Spirit,
> The holy church,
> The forgiveness of sins,
> The resurrection of the body
> And everlasting life.

Let us examine these beliefs line by line.

(a) *I believe in God almighty*

Christians are not alone in believing in God. Jews believe in Yahweh, the God of the Old Testament, and Muslims believe in Allah. Despite these different names, Christians, Jews and Muslims all believe in the Supreme Being who is greater than man and watches over the life of men. He is the Supreme Being because there can be nothing greater than God. He has created the world and he is responsible at all times, at this very moment, for maintaining it in existence. If God did not exist nothing would exist. God is all powerful and he represents everything that is good. We do not directly experience God—we do not see him or hear him—but we do not think that he is remote and distant because of this. Jesus Christ told men to address God as 'Father', as in the Lord's Prayer: 'Our Father in heaven . . .'. The word he used was the equivalent of 'dad'; it was a term of affection. St Paul says that when we address God as 'Father' it shows that we are his children (*Romans*, Ch. 8, vv. 15–16). We call him Father because he has all the characteristics of a human father: he protects us, he leads us to maturity, he is responsible for our existence and well-being. But he is more powerful, more caring and wiser than any human father could be. In addition he is directly involved in what happens to people in their lives and he has shown this in Jesus of Nazareth.

(b) *I believe in Jesus Christ, his only son, our Lord*
In his own language, Hebrew, Jesus's name was Joshua, but when this was translated into Greek and then into English it came out as Jesus. Christ, on the other hand, is not a personal name but a title. It comes from the Greek for Messiah, the Hebrew word which means 'the anointed one'. King David and all the kings of the Old Testament were anointed with oil (just as the kings and queens of England still are at their coronation). The Messiah was the king that the Jews were waiting for to liberate them from their enemies. Christians believe that God's Messiah has come and that Jesus of Nazareth is that Messiah. Jesus is the man that God has sent to free them from everything that threatens them and makes life unbearable. He is their liberator and Christians believe that their life is a life of freedom. Jesus is the Son of God because, just as an ordinary son looks like his father, so Jesus shows us what God the Father is like. Christians also call him 'Lord' because they see him as their master and teacher: they can follow his example and learn from him. They are his pupils.

(c) *He was born of the Holy Spirit and the Virgin Mary*
The opening of the Gospels of Matthew and Luke tell us that Jesus was born in Bethlehem, a small town in Palestine, when it was part of the Roman Empire and when it was being ruled by King Herod the Great. According to Roman historical records Herod died in 4 BC, so Jesus must have been born a short while before that, perhaps in 6 BC. His parents were Joseph and a girl called Mary, both of whom came from Nazareth, a town to the north of Jerusalem. Jesus's birth was not very respectable because although Joseph and Mary were engaged, Jesus was conceived before they were actually married. In fact, in certain respects Jesus's life was not particularly respectable; although he did not approve of their behaviour, he mixed with thieves and prostitutes and was finally executed as a criminal.

When the creed says that the Holy Spirit and the Virgin Mary were responsible for Jesus's conception, many Christians believe that Mary was actually a virgin and had not had sexual relations with Joseph; others find this difficult to believe. But the important thing is the belief that the Spirit of God was present at Jesus's conception and birth. There was something special about Jesus even from the moment of his birth.

(d) *He was crucified under Pontius Pilate and was buried*
Pontius Pilate was a Roman soldier who was Governor of Palestine from AD 26 to 36. One spring during this period, when he was in Jerusalem for the Jewish Passover feast, Pilate had to judge Jesus when a criminal charge was brought against him by some Jews on the grounds of encouraging political rebellion. He found Jesus guilty and executed him by the most appalling of methods: Jesus was tortured and nailed to a cross to die of exhaustion and suffocation. Jesus died. He was not unconscious. He was dead and his corpse was sealed inside a stone tomb. His disciples were broken men; they must have thought that this was the end of everything for them.

(e) *On the third day he rose from the dead*
But Christians believe that it was not the end, for three days later Jesus's tomb was found to be empty and he appeared, alive, to his disciples. He had been given a new life by God. The word normally

Matthias Grünewald painted four crucifixions in the sixteenth century. One has been lost, and one is in Washington. The third, painted by 1516, is part of an altar piece of eleven wooden panels. It was painted for the chapel of a hospital at Isenheim in France and expresses for the patients the reality of the suffering of Christ. The picture above is now at Karlsruhe, West Germany.

used to describe what happened to Jesus in the tomb is *resurrection*. The Greek words which occur in the New Testament simply mean 'to stand up' or 'to wake up'. The Gospels describe how Jesus was seen by Mary Magdalene, by the Apostles and by many of the first Christians; how he talked with them and ate with them. Christians are convinced that the death of Jesus was not the end of him. He had a future beyond the grave and Christians believe that his influence can be felt directly in the present.

Belief in the continued life of Jesus has a further significance. Before his death Jesus was obviously a very remarkable man, as we can see from his teaching as it is recorded in the Gospels. But if God has continued his life beyond the grave, this is God's confirmation that Jesus is his son, his Messiah, and that Jesus's teaching is God's teaching. It is a confirmation that we should lead our lives by following the example of Jesus of Nazareth.

(f) *He ascended into heaven and sits at the right hand of the Father*

When this line was written in the fourth century everyone believed that the earth was flat and that heaven was a place up above it. Later they discovered that this was not so. When Christians say that Jesus has ascended into heaven they do not mean that he is in a place up above. They mean two things. First, that he is no longer bodily present with us, he is absent, he has gone away. And secondly, that he has been exalted above the human race and that he now shares the life of God his Father, the creator of all men.

Traditionally, when a man holds a banquet or a dinner for his friends, the place of honour is the seat on his right. When the creed says that Jesus sits at the right hand of the Father it simply means that of all men Jesus holds the place of honour in God's presence.

(g) *From where he will come to judge the living and the dead*

Christians believe that just as Jesus was the representative of God on earth during his lifetime, so he will act on behalf of God in heaven. Christians accepted the Jewish belief that God will bring the course of history to a halt at some unknown time in the future. At the end of history Jesus Christ will judge people on what they have done with their lives, whether they have accepted or rejected God and Jesus Christ. This line of the creed states that all people will be judged, both those who are still alive at the end of time and those who have died. All those who have accepted Jesus of Nazareth in their lifetime will be raised up just as Jesus himself was. An early Christian image of the final judgment can be found in *Matthew*, Ch. 25, vv. 31–46. Not all Christians would now accept this early belief in the end of time, the general resurrection and the final judgment, but all Christians do believe that they are accountable to God for their beliefs and their actions.

(h) *I believe in the Holy Spirit*

When we talk about God we address him as 'he' as though he were a man. But people who believe in God do not think that he is really a man with a body. God is *not* an old man with a long white beard, but *any* picture we have of him will be a distortion of his real nature. Religious people believe that God is spirit, because anything with a body is limited and God has no limits. *Genesis* describes God as a spirit when it says that at the creation of the world 'the spirit of God moved over the waters of chaos'. The spirit is the creative power of God; it is that which gives life. When Jesus was baptised by John, the spirit of God rested on him, and there the spirit is pictured as a dove (*Mark*, Ch. 1, vv. 9–11).

The Holy Spirit is the continued presence of Jesus after he had left his disciples. The *Acts of the Apostles* pictures the coming of the Spirit to the Apostles by wind and flames (*Acts*, Ch. 2, vv. 1–4). Spirit means wind or breath. The Holy Spirit is the breath of God which creates new life. If you want to know what were the gifts of the Holy Spirit for the early Christians, look at *1 Corinthians*, Ch. 12, vv. 3–11. St Paul also thought that the Spirit helps people to pray when they do not know what they want to say (*Romans*, Ch. 8, vv. 26–27).

(i) *I believe in the holy church*

The later version of this creed says 'the holy catholic church'. The Church is the totality of all Christians under the headship of Jesus Christ. 'Holy' means 'different' or 'separate': Christians have been called by God to live a different kind of life dedicated to him. Remember that in this sense the Church is not a building, it is the community of all Christians. 'Catholic' originally meant 'universal' so the catholic church is the universal church and it includes all Christians. Often Catholic Church is used as an abbreviation of Roman Catholic Church. While this is a convenient way of speaking, it should be remembered that the universal church includes all Christians both inside and outside the Roman Catholic Church. Normally entry into the Church is by baptism. This is a ceremony in which a person is symbolically washed in water as a sign of their decision to live a new life. Until quite recently a large proportion of babies died soon after their birth and Christian parents became anxious about the fate of these unbaptised children who had died. As a result of this anxiety, it became the common practice after about AD 400 for parents to baptise their children while they were still babies and they promised to bring up their children as Christians until they could decide for themselves.

(j) *I believe in the forgiveness of sins*
Sin is an offence committed against God. If Christians share the Spirit of God, then when they do something seriously wrong they are not just offending some other person but they have broken their relationship with God. Christians believe that all men are sinful, that they are corrupt and are capable of great evil. Just think of all the people who have been murdered, massacred and tortured this century and of the brutality which will be taking place somewhere in the world at this very moment. Think of all the examples of petty nastiness we experience every day. Men are not always sinful, but everyone is at some time or other. The fact that men are corrupt and lower than God is symbolised in *Genesis* when Adam (Adam is the Hebrew word for 'man'; he is a symbol for the human race) eats the apple given to him by Eve and loses his innocence. But Christians believe that despite the fact that men are sinful God has the power and the willingness to forgive us our offences: see, for example, *1 John*, Ch. 1, vv. 8–9, 'If we say we have no sin, we deceive ourselves, and the truth is not in us. If we confess our sins, he is faithful and just, and will forgive our sins and cleanse us from all unrighteousness.'

(k) *I believe in the resurrection of the body and everlasting life*
The belief that Jesus has been raised from the dead and that we too will be raised at the end of time is at the centre of Christian belief.

A long piece of linen kept in Turin Cathedral is said to have been the shroud wrapped round Jesus in the tomb. There are indistinct marks on the shroud which were photographed at the end of last century and the negative shows that they are the imprint of a body with blood stains. The peculiarities of the imprint show that it was made by the body of a Jew who had been crucified. The face is shown above in the photographic negative. Many believe this to be the face of Jesus, but we cannot be certain of this.

There is, however, a good deal of disagreement about how this belief is to be understood. The traditional belief is that Jesus's own body was raised after his death and that his Apostles saw him, spoke with him and ate with him. These meetings are described at the end of the Gospels (except Mark's Gospel). Jesus's new bodily life, moreover, was a transformed life; he had become immortal, incorruptible, glorified, and he had what St Paul called a 'spiritual body' rather than a mere physical body. But he was recognisably the same Jesus. Christians believe that we can already share that new risen life of Jesus in part through faith. And traditionally Christians have believed that at the end of time our bodies will be recreated, transformed and raised up like Jesus Christ himself, and that we will not die any more. Other Christians, however, prefer a more spiritual interpretation of the resurrection and see it in terms of the immortality of the soul. They consider that belief in a risen body is the product of a primitive mentality with which we need no longer agree.

Christians do agree, however, that we can share the risen life of Jesus. Just as Jesus has continued his life beyond the grave, the creed says that all other men can share this life if they believe that God can do it for them. St Paul said exactly this when he wrote: 'For I am sure that neither death nor life . . . nor things present nor things to come, nor anything else in all creation, will be able to separate us from the love of God in Christ Jesus our Lord.' (*Romans*, Ch. 8, vv. 38–39)

The basis for all these beliefs can be found in various parts of the New Testament, but a creed is an attempt to summarise the basic beliefs that all Christians share through all ages. This is the reason why Christians still recite publicly this very old creed. Later we shall look at the differences of belief and practice that we find in the different Churches of Christianity. But always bear in mind that all Christians share these fundamental beliefs about God and Jesus Christ.

1 In what ways is God similar to a human person? In what ways is he unlike a human person? What qualities does God have in the picture on p. 18? When you think of God, do you imagine him to be like that picture?

2 Read *Exodus*, Ch. 20, vv. 1–5. Why, do you think, were the Jews commanded not to make images and pictures of God?
3 When a famous person dies, newspapers publish an 'obituary' which is a brief summary of that person's life and achievements. Compose your own obituary of Jesus, using this book, the Gospels, your memory and your imagination.
4 If you had been asked, would you have become one of Jesus's disciples? Give your reasons.
5 Read *1 Corinthians*, Ch. 15, vv. 3–8, *Luke*, Ch. 24, vv. 1–43 and *John*, Ch. 20, vv. 1–18. Give a summary of how Jesus showed himself after his resurrection and decide, if you are able, whether this is convincing historical evidence for the resurrection. How would an historian react to this?
6 If you had been a disciple and had been told that Jesus had risen from the dead, how would you have reacted? See how one of the disciples reacted in *John*, Ch. 20, vv. 19–29.
7 What effect did the Holy Spirit have on the first Christians? Look at these passages: *Acts*, Ch. 2, vv. 1–12, *1 Corinthians*, Ch. 12, vv. 3–11, *Romans*, Ch. 12, vv. 6–8, Ch. 8, vv. 26–27, *John*, Ch. 14, vv. 25–26.
8 What is meant by 'sin'? Why is forgiveness important?
9 A film is available from Concord Films called *It's About This Carpenter* (14 mins, black and white). Its distributors say: 'A carpenter delivers a cross to a New York church. Reactions to him vary: some people find the sight humorous, some are antagonistic, and some ignore him.'

4

The Roman Catholic Church

The Roman Catholic Church is the oldest of the Churches in the West and became separate from the Eastern Orthodox Churches in 1054. This split came after almost ten centuries of unity and although agreements for reunion were made in the thirteenth and fifteenth centuries, they never had any effect.

Roman Catholics trace the origin of their Church back to the Apostles. Historically all other Churches have broken away from the Roman Catholic Church because they disapproved of some of the things it taught and did. It is still the biggest Church. There are about 700 million Catholics (as we shall now call them) and they are to be found in every country of the world, though there are relatively few in a country like China. Catholicism is strongest numerically in Ireland, Spain and Portugal in Western Europe, Poland and Hungary in Eastern Europe, and in South America. There are about 50 million Catholics in the United States (a quarter of the population) and about four million in Britain (about one twelfth of the population).

Britain was a Catholic country until the time of the Reformation (see Chapter 2) but Catholicism was reintroduced into Britain by Irish immigrants only in the nineteenth century. However, a few wealthy families, like the Duke of Norfolk's family, who could afford to pay the fines imposed by Queen Elizabeth I, stayed Catholic right through this period. And the Reformation never reached as far as the small islands of the Outer Hebrides.

What is it that unites all these Christians in a single denomination? As their name 'Roman Catholic' implies, they believe that the Pope, who is the Bishop of Rome, is the Head of the Church on earth. Of course, Jesus Christ is the Head of the Church, but Catholics believe that the Bishop of Rome is his representative. He is the one who is responsible for organising the Church and taking its major decisions.

Karol Wojtyla, former Archbishop of Krakow, Poland, became the 258th Pope in 1978 when he took the name John Paul II.

Catholics believe that the first Bishop of Rome was St Peter. When Catholics explain why they believe that the Bishop of Rome is the Head of the Church they try to show how Peter was the chief of the Apostles and they usually refer to Jesus's words in *Matthew*, Ch. 16, v. 18: 'You are Peter and on this rock I will build my Church, and the powers of death will not prevail against it. I will give you the keys of the kingdom of heaven, and whatever you bind on earth will be bound in heaven, and whatever you forgive on earth will be forgiven in heaven.' It is generally believed that Peter went to Rome in the last years of his life and that he was killed there by Nero in AD 65 together with St Paul. It is thought that in those last years of his life he was the head or bishop of the small community of Christians in Rome. And Catholics believe that Peter's position as head of all the Church has been passed on to all later Bishops of Rome, right down to the present day. Protestants reject this belief and dislike the way that Popes have sometimes misused their authority in the past. There has been one English Pope; Nicholas Breakspear became Hadrian IV in the twelfth century.

The Catholic Church is made up of ordinary (or 'lay') people and priests. Priests are the representatives of lay Catholics in religious matters. They have responsibility for a *parish*, and within that small area they have the job of celebrating services, preaching, teaching and visiting people. The law of the Church has for many centuries forbidden priests from marrying. In each local district—known as a *diocese*—there is a bishop who is the organiser of that diocese. The bishops are the successors of the Apostles just as the Pope is the successor of Peter. Each country will have a number of dioceses and will be self-governing in most ordinary matters. Each country will also have one (or perhaps several) cardinals in charge. 'Cardinal' is an honorary title given to a small number of male Catholics. They are usually bishops but they do not have to be. There are about 140 at the moment. The head of the Catholic Church in England and Wales in 1983 was Cardinal Basil Hume. The cardinals of the Church are responsible for electing the Pope. When a Pope dies, the cardinals are locked in a wing of the Vatican in Rome and, like a jury during a serious trial, they do not come out until they have selected a successor.

The bishops of the Roman Catholic Church meet in St Peter's, Rome.

When they have selected a new Pope, they show this to the crowds outside by burning the ballot papers to send white smoke through a chimney. A short while later his name is announced from a balcony in the Vatican.

Important decisions about belief and practice which affect all Catholics are taken in Rome and periodically bishops from every country meet there to discuss matters of importance. Very occasionally, when the Church faces a crisis, all the bishops meet in what is known as an Ecumenical Council. The first was held at Nicaea in Asia Minor in AD 325, and the most recent—the twenty-first—was held in the Vatican in Rome between 1962 and 1965. The crisis which provoked this council was the question of how the Church should come to terms with the modern world in preaching the message of Jesus Christ.

The council was called by the most remarkable Catholic the world has seen for a long time, *Pope John XXIII*. When Pius XII died in 1958, there was no obvious successor for the job. The cardinals decided to elect an old man who would not do any harm and who would die after a few years when, it was thought, a successor would be ready for the position. The old man—he was 76—was

Pope John XXIII

Angelo Roncalli, Bishop of Venice, who had come to Rome for the election, having bought a return ticket as he did not expect to stay long. To everyone's surprise, especially his own, he never needed the return half of the ticket. But this man, who was expected to keep quiet and do nothing, decided that the Church was out of date and out of touch with the problems of the modern world. Pope John, as he now called himself, was responsible for introducing widespread changes into the Catholic Church and he called a council of all 2000 bishops to discuss the problems faced by the Church. Of the many changes introduced, the most noticeable was that for the first time since the Middle Ages Latin was no longer used as a kind of international language in church services. Pope John made both friends and enemies in calling for such changes, and he died before the council had finished its work. But because of him the Catholic Church will never be quite the same again.

Roman Catholic religious practice is based on the seven *sacraments*. A sacrament is a form of ritual in which a person acts out his relationship with God. The first of these is *baptism*. This is the sacrament of entry into the Church in which a person is symbolically washed in water as a sign of the forgiveness of all previous sin. It is in baptism that a person is made a Christian and so baptism has become known as a person's 'christening'. It is usually babies that are baptised, but adults are baptised if they become Christian later in life.

The second sacrament is *confirmation*. When boys and girls around the age of twelve are blessed by the bishop, their faith is 'confirmed' by him and they become adult members of the Church.

The other sacraments include *penance* or confession when a person privately confesses his or her sins and receives absolution or forgiveness from a priest, who acts as God's representative. There is *marriage* when two people promise to live together for the rest of their lives in a relationship of love and fidelity. *Ordination* is when a man is blessed by his bishop and is made a priest. There is the sacrament of *healing*, often called the last rites, given to people who are close to death. This includes an anointing with oil, confession and communion, and various prayers for the recovery of the person.

The most common of all Catholic services is the *mass*, during which the sacrament of the holy eucharist is celebrated. (*Eucharist* is from the Greek word meaning 'to offer thanks'.) In every Catholic church there will be a mass on every day of the week and several on Sundays. Different forms of this service are to be found in other Christian Churches and it is known by various names, including *holy communion* and *the Lord's supper*. It is the service in which the priest repeats the words and actions of Jesus at the last supper he took with his disciples in Jerusalem just before he was killed. The word 'mass' is derived from something the priest said at the end of the old Latin mass, 'ite, missa est', which means 'go, it is finished', to which the people replied 'Deo gratias', 'thanks be to God'. So this service has become known in Latin and Italian as the *missa*, in German as *die Messe*, in French as *la messe*, and in all English-speaking countries as *the mass*.

When a priest says mass he puts on the traditional vestments. These include a long white robe known as an *alb*, which is tied with a cord round the middle; a *stole*, a long cloth band which goes round the neck and hangs down the front; and a *chasuble* which goes over the head and shoulders like a large Mexican poncho. The colours of some of these vestments change from season to season; purple is the penitential colour for Advent and Lent, white for Christmas and Easter, red for Pentecost or Whitsuntide, and green for most of the rest of the year. Black is worn at funerals. Some of the prayers of the mass are the same all the time but some change from day to day as different festivals are celebrated. The mass begins with a prayer for forgiveness, followed by the prayer for the day and three readings from the Bible. Then the creed is recited or sung and on Sundays there will be a sermon. After that the mass follows the last supper of Jesus with the addition of various prayers. The priest blesses or consecrates small pieces of white bread which have been made without yeast (like the 'unleavened bread' of the Jewish Passover feast) and he consecrates wine in a silver cup known as a *chalice*. Then the priest and people share communion, or the common meal, by eating the bread. (Only the priest sips the wine.)

When the priest consecrates the bread and wine, he repeats the words of Jesus: 'This is my body. This cup is the new covenant in my blood. Do this, as often as you drink it, in memory of me.' So the mass is a remembrance of the death of Jesus. Catholics believe that, in some real sense, when they eat the bread and drink the wine, they are eating and drinking the body and blood of Jesus Christ. He is present with them when they eat and drink.

If you go into a Catholic church, you will see the altar near the end of the church and on it there will be two or possibly six candlesticks and a crucifix. There is likely to be a *confessional* at the back of the church where people may make their confession. A confessional is a pair of wooden cubicles separated by a partition. The priest sits in one and listens through a grille in the partition to the confession of the sins of the individual who kneels on the other side of the partition. This is where the sacrament of penance takes place (see page 33) and where the priest can offer advice to the individual. This complicated arrangement maintains the privacy of what is said and hides the identity of the person making the confession. The priest will not

Children come for communion at Sunday mass in a Catholic parish.

usually know who is making the confession and he may not under any circumstances repeat what he has heard.

You will probably also see some statues, perhaps of Jesus, of Mary his mother, or of some saints. These are images to remind Catholics of some holy person. A *saint* is a man or woman who has been declared by the Church to have been particularly holy, someone who is an example of what all Christians should be. The greatest of all these saints of course is Mary, who is the mother of Jesus Christ, and her importance is recognised in a number of festivals in the Catholic Church. Catholics have a tradition of praying to Mary and the saints, of whom these statues are reminders. Just as Christians often pray for each other, so Catholics ask Mary and the saints to pray on their behalf for their needs.

We have already seen that in the Catholic Church there are priests and lay people. There are also many *monks* and *nuns* in Religious Orders. These are people who have decided to devote their lives entirely to the service of God. Sometimes they devote themselves to a life of silence and prayer in a monastery (men who do this are known as monks), and sometimes to a life of study or a life of activity such as missionary work, teaching, nursing or something of that sort. (Men who do that are usually known as friars—from the Latin *fratres* meaning 'brothers'.) After a trial period a person who decides to join a Religious Order will take three vows—a vow of *poverty*, a vow to live a life of *celibacy* (i.e. not to get married) and a vow of *obedience* to God and to his religious superior.

There are a great many religious orders. The best known often take the name of their founder. The Benedictines are monks who follow the example of St Benedict by living a life of prayer. The Franciscans are friars who live a life of poverty like St Francis. The Dominicans were founded by St Dominic; they are properly known as the Order of Preachers and they devote themselves to studying theology, preaching and teaching. Perhaps the best-known order is the Society of Jesus (whose members are known as the Jesuits) which was founded by St Ignatius Loyola just after the Reformation. The members of almost all these religious orders live in small communities and they meet several times each day to pray together. For the rest of the time they do the work they have chosen to do.

All these religious orders were founded in the past when some particular job needed to be done. The best modern example is not a religious order but a group of priests, mainly in France, who in the last 25 years have felt the need to leave their parishes which they thought were becoming increasingly irrelevant. These men decided to take ordinary manual jobs while doing their work as priests in their spare time. They are known as *worker priests*. What they have been trying to do is very important but the movement has not yet been a success because they have made a lot of enemies. Some bishops and priests have opposed them because the worker priests have claimed that the traditional parish is irrelevant. And many employers have disliked them because they tend to be politically left wing and have been intelligent and hard-working enough to organise workers into opposing unjust working conditions. They have given up organising their parishes and have in some cases begun organising strikes.

Perhaps the biggest problem facing the Catholic Church today is what position it is to take in those countries where there are repressive military governments and where liberation movements are trying to overthrow them. The question is whether the Church must always be opposed to all forms of violence or whether the Church can accept

Helder Camara

that some forms of violence are regrettable but necessary. This is a very serious difficulty in South America where there are 300 million Catholics and where a great many of the governments are oppressive military dictatorships. Christians face the same problem with racialist governments in southern Africa. Catholics may want to see these governments changed but should they support violence in doing this or not? Two well-known South American Catholics represent opposing views.

The Brazilian Archbishop Helder Camara lives in the north-east of Brazil which is extremely poor, where there is a lot of disease and which is largely ignored by the military government. Helder Camara is an opponent of the government; however, he is completely opposed to violence because he thinks that it can only lead to more violence and does not finally solve anyone's problems. He has been nominated as a candidate for the Nobel Peace Prize and would almost certainly have won it had it not been for political pressure brought by the Brazilian and United States governments.

In contrast, Camilo Torres, a priest from Colombia, left his parish in 1966 to join a group of guerrilla fighters. He thought that the only way to create a decent life for people in Colombia was to bring in a socialist government, and that this could only be achieved by overthrowing the existing government as was done in Cuba some years ago. He was killed by the army a few months later.

Camara and Torres are both examples of Catholics who are trying to make it possible for ordinary people to live decent human lives. Which of these examples Catholics in South America and the rest of the world will follow remains to be seen.

1 Explain why Roman Catholics believe that the Pope is the Head of the Church.
2 Who is the present Pope? What is his role in the Roman Catholic Church?
3 Describe the seven sacraments. Do you think they are useful and important? Could any of them be dispensed with?
4 Try to visit a Catholic church. If it is possible for your group to visit the church together, arrange for the parish priest to show you round and answer any questions you may have.
5 Try to talk to a Catholic priest (or ask one to talk to your class) about his beliefs and his work.
6 What is your reaction to the views of Helder Camara and Camilo Torres? Do you think Christians should be involved in politics to try to change society?

You can discover something about Helder Camara by reading the book on him by Neville Cheetham in the series *People With a Purpose*, edited by Ian Birnie.
7 Two films are available from Concord Films: *Giovanni* about the life of John XXIII (colour, 50 mins, 1972), and *A Threat to the State* about the political role of some Catholic priests in Brazil (a Granada 'World in Action' film, colour, 30 mins, 1973).

5

The Church of England

The Church of England began its existence at the beginning of the sixteenth century as a protest movement against the Catholic Church as it existed at that time. It is, however, different from many of the other Protestant Churches in that it is governed by bishops, like the Roman Catholic Church, and because of this the Church of England still regards itself as part of the Catholic Church—though not of the Roman Catholic Church. Since the time of the Reformation it has been the main Church in England and it is a national Church which is independent of all other Churches abroad.

As we have already discovered, Christianity was officially brought to England in 597 by St Augustine, who became the first Archbishop of Canterbury. Throughout the Middle Ages the Church in England was a part of the Catholic Church in Europe which had the Pope as its Head. In 1517 a widespread protest movement broke out in northern Europe against abuses in the Catholic Church. Martin Luther, as we have seen, organised this movement in Germany. At first Henry VIII defended the Pope against the attack by Luther; he even wrote a book—though not a very good one—in which he argued against Luther. For this Pope Leo X gave Henry the title *fidei defensor*, 'defender of the faith', and the letters 'F.D.' can still be seen on British coins after the king or queen's name. However, when Henry's request for a divorce from his wife Catherine was turned down by the next Pope, Clement VII, Henry declared that the Church of England was to be independent of the Pope and the Catholic Church in Europe, and he made himself the Head of the Church in place of the Pope. After Henry's death and the brief reign of Edward VI, Queen Mary Tudor tried to make England a Roman Catholic country once more but she failed. Her successor, Queen Elizabeth I, made sure that England was a Protestant country but she tried to follow a middle

path between Rome on the one hand and continental Protestantism on the other. Ever since that time the monarch of England has been the official Head of the Church of England. Even today it is the Queen and her Prime Minister who choose the bishops of the Church of England. In addition, whenever the Church of England wants to make a change in its prayer book, a law must be passed in Parliament to allow it, though there has recently been a move to modify this.

How does the Church of England differ from the Roman Catholic Church? Before the Reformation the Catholic Church in England was ruled by bishops, but they were appointed by the Pope and they looked to Rome as the final authority in the Church. Before Henry VIII, other kings of England had come into conflict with Rome: Henry II, for example, who caused the death of Archbishop Thomas Beckett, and King John who was excommunicated in 1209. Taxes were paid every year to help pay the expenses of the Church in Rome, and a good deal of land in England was owned by the Church and by monasteries. After 1533 Henry had broken completely with Rome, so he appointed his own bishops, stopped all Church taxes being sent to Rome, solved all legal matters (such as his divorce) by himself, destroyed all the monasteries and gave Church land to his friends.

Despite all this, however, much remained the same. The Church was still ruled (after the King) by bishops, with Canterbury and York as the two chief Bishops. Parishes were still looked after by their priests; the churches and cathedrals of England still performed their daily and weekly services. But the Church of England was independent and, under the guidance of the monarch and of Parliament, could control its own affairs, as it still does today.

The first main difference that the ordinary people would have noticed after the Reformation was that church services were, for the first time, in English. The Roman Catholic mass and other services were changed in many ways but the main task was to translate them from Latin into English. The job of translation was given to *Thomas Cranmer* (left), the first Archbishop of Canterbury after the English Reformation. He produced the *Book of Common Prayer* in which you will find the words of all the services of the Church of England, and which is still used in Anglican churches today. Here is a prayer written by Cranmer:

> Blessed Lord, who hast caused all holy Scriptures to be written for our learning: grant that we may in such wise hear them, read, mark, learn, and inwardly digest them, that by patience and comfort of thy holy Word, we may embrace and ever hold fast the blessed hope of everlasting life, which thou hast given us in our Saviour Jesus Christ. Amen.

This is a prayer that God will help us to read the Bible attentively and it is read in Anglican churches two weeks before Christmas. If you look at the prayer carefully, you will notice that it is written in very fine poetic language, but that the language is very dated. Since it is over 400 years old, you may well find its meaning difficult to grasp at a first reading. This is the problem with the Book of Common Prayer. It is so well written that no one is likely to write anything so good again, and yet it no longer contains the language of everyday speech as it once did.

The Prayer Book contains a number of statements, known as the *Thirty Nine Articles*, which summarise the beliefs of the Church of England, though these are mainly concerned with controversies of the sixteenth century. It also contains the words of the services of the Church of England. What are these services? By far the most common service in a Catholic church is the mass, the repetition of the last supper of Jesus. The Anglican Church has the same service though in a slightly different form, and here it is called *Holy Communion* or the *Eucharist*. The Catholic mass is celebrated much more frequently, however, as most Catholic churches will have three, four or even five masses each Sunday with an additional mass each day of the week. An Anglican church may only have two or perhaps three communion services in a week, one or occasionally two on a Sunday and another in the middle of the week. The priest wears vestments which are simpler and less colourful than those of a Catholic priest. He normally wears a white *surplice* over a long black *cassock*. At Holy Communion bread and wine are blessed and given to the congregation. The main services, however, are Morning Prayer and Evening Prayer which are made up of hymns, prayers, readings from the Bible and a sermon. These services are celebrated publicly each Sunday morning and evening and every Anglican priest has to say the prayers of Morning Prayer and Evening Prayer each day. The important point about these services is that everyone should participate actively.

An Anglican priest.

The inside of Anglican churches varies considerably, but usually they are much simpler than Roman Catholic churches. At the far end of the church, probably beneath a stained glass window, there will be a simple wooden altar covered with a decorated cloth. On the altar there will be a cross and two candlesticks. It is on this altar that the bread and wine of Holy Communion are consecrated. Further down the church there will be *choirstalls*—seats for the choir—a *pulpit* and a *lectern* (reading stand) on which will be placed a Bible. It is unlikely that there will be any statues as in a Catholic church; the Bible has taken their place. Nor will you see a confessional. As with most other churches, you are likely to find it decorated with flowers.

The first contact many people have with the Church of England is with their local vicar. Wherever you live—if you live in England—there will be a Church of England priest who is responsible for the area in which you live. He may have visited your home and he may occasionally visit your school. Every priest in the

Church of England has to undergo several years of training. Either he will have been at a university for three years and at a theological college for two years, or he will have followed a four-year course at a theological college. These colleges are paid for by the Church and the students study a variety of subjects which will prepare them for their work as a parish priest. Similar courses are taken by priests and ministers from all other Churches. At the end of his course the student will be made a *deacon* by his bishop. He will then go to work in a parish for one year under the supervision of a parish priest. During this period he can preach and hold services but he cannot celebrate Holy Communion. If he completes his year of apprenticeship successfully, the deacon is ordained by his bishop and becomes a *priest*.

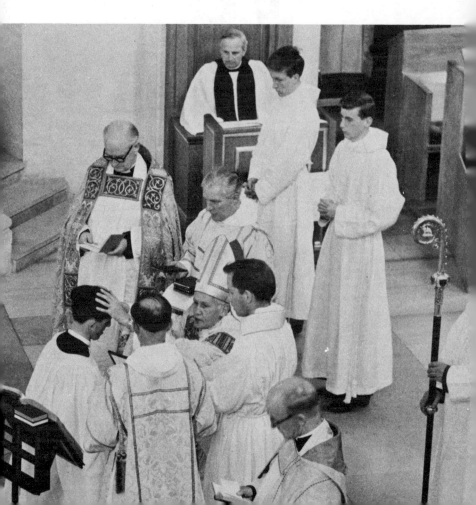

From this time a priest can celebrate all services and can run a parish by himself. The whole country is divided into 43 districts known as *dioceses*, and in each diocese there is one man who is made a *bishop* who acts as the head of the district. Each bishop has a cathedral which is the chief church of that diocese. This form of organisation, as you will now realise, is just like that of the Roman Catholic Church.

For 300 years the Church of England was a national Church which was completely independent of all other Churches. In the nineteenth century, however, as the British Empire spread across the globe, the Church of England sent missionaries abroad to preach the message of Jesus Christ. Over the last hundred years or more the Church of England has spread to parts of Africa, the West Indies, Australia and New Zealand, India and some other parts of Asia, as well as to places like Gibraltar and Jerusalem. The Anglican Church also has strong associations with the Episcopal Church in the United States and in Canada and Scotland. This association of Churches is known as the *Anglican Communion*. In England about half the population has been baptised in the Church of England, but only two or three million of these are practising Anglicans—that is, they go to church at least at Easter and Christmas. The Anglican Communion, however, has about 40 million practising members, many of them in the United States where 60 per cent of the population goes to church regularly.

The Anglican Church in each of these countries has priests and bishops. Each country also nominates one or two of its bishops to become *archbishops*. There are two of these in England, at Canterbury and York. John Habgood became Archbishop of York in 1983. The 102nd Archbishop of Canterbury, Robert Runcie, took up his position in 1980. The two archbishops and the twenty most senior bishops of the Church of England are allowed to sit in Parliament in the House of Lords.

Perhaps the best known of the English bishops is Trevor Huddleston. He is a member of a religious community in Yorkshire, the Community of the Resurrection. In the 1940s he went to work in South Africa among black Africans, many of whom live a miserable life. While he was there he drew the attention of the world to these miseries in a book called *Naught For Your Comfort* and gave lectures in many countries on life in South Africa. While he was in South Africa he

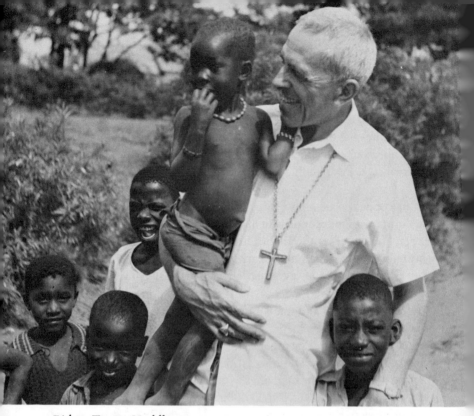

Bishop Trevor Huddleston

was constantly persecuted by the police and government because of the work he did with Africans. After working in other parts of Africa he finally left because he thought that the Africans should be allowed and encouraged to run their own Church. Since he came back he has become one of the most popular bishops in the Church of England.

The Church of England has recently found itself in a serious financial situation. The funds the Church has available for paying its priests will not stretch to pay salaries which can keep up with the increased cost of living. A lot of Anglican priests now find it very hard to make ends meet. This is a problem which faces many priests and ministers in Britain today. In addition, many Anglican churches were built centuries ago in the countryside when most people still worked on farms. After the Industrial Revolution in the nineteenth century, much of the population moved into the cities, but a large proportion of Anglican churches are in the country away from the centres of population. These are often very beautiful buildings but how is the Church of England to pay for their upkeep? And how can it spare priests to look after them when they are needed in city parishes?

A recent argument in the Church of England has concerned the ordination of women. Some Churches in the Anglican Communion have recently ordained women as priests, but the majority of priests in the Church of England are opposed to this. The bishops now have to decide whether they should recognise these women as priests or whether they should follow the tradition of the Roman Catholic Church and the Eastern Orthodox Churches who have never ordained women. The outcome of this issue could affect the future reunion of the Christian Churches more than any other.

1 What is the Anglican Communion?
2 Most people still marry in Church of England churches. Read the marriage service in the Book of Common Prayer. Do you agree with the way marriage is described there as a permanent relationship which has to be preserved through thick and thin? If you would like to see the language rewritten in a modern style, how would you rewrite the marriage vows?
3 Find out about your own diocese and write a brief account of it. Include: its name, the area it covers and the name of your bishop. If you can, and are interested, find out about the history of the diocese and its cathedral.
4 Trevor Huddleston's work in South Africa is described by Ian Birnie in the series *People With A Purpose*. Read this book and write a short description of the work Huddleston did in Africa.
5 If your teacher can arrange for a Church of England priest to visit your class, question him about his beliefs and the work he does.
6 It is possible to hire a number of films which deal with various aspects of the Church of England from The National Society for Promoting Religious Education, Church House, Dean's Yard, Westminster, London SW1P 3NZ.

6

The Methodist Church

From the beginning of the Reformation there were disagreements among the Protestant reformers. Various Protestant Churches went their own separate ways and these divisions were also to be found in Britain. In England, however, most of these divisions arose because some Protestants refused to conform to the insistence of Elizabeth I that all Englishmen should be members of the Church of England. The Nonconformist Churches in Britain have a similar view of Christianity but a number of small differences have kept them apart from each other. We shall now examine one of these Nonconformist Churches in detail, the Methodist Church, because of its close connection with the Church of England and because it is typical of the whole group even though it had its beginning more than 200 years after the Reformation. In the next chapter we shall then have a briefer look at some of the other Nonconformist Churches.

The Methodist Church originated with a group of men in Oxford in the early part of the eighteenth century. They had been brought together by the brothers *John* and *Charles Wesley*. John Wesley (shown preaching opposite), a priest in the Church of England, thought that it had lost touch with God and with the people, and he wanted to restore the enthusiasm and spontaneity of the Church of the first century. He tried to do this by studying Greek and the Greek New Testament in order to understand what the early Christians thought and how they behaved. Wesley's group revived customs of earlier times by fasting and by going to communion more frequently than was customary at that time. They became known as 'The Holy Club', 'The Bible Moths' and 'The Methodists' because they were so methodical in their habits. It was this last nickname that stuck and people said of them,

> By rule they eat, by rule they drink,
> Do all things else by rule, but think—
> Method alone must guide 'em all,
> Whence Methodists themselves they call.

So Methodism began as a small reform group within the Church of England and it was only much later that it expanded and broke away as a Church in its own right.

In addition to their purely religious activities, the Oxford Methodists ran a school for the poor and distributed food, clothes, medicine and books. One of them was William Morgan who started visiting prisoners. He wrote letters for the illiterate and taught them how to read and write their own letters.

In 1735, when America was still a British colony, John and Charles Wesley set sail on a missionary journey to Georgia. While John was on the ship he contacted a group of Moravians, a community of German Protestants. After having learnt some German, he discovered that among their beliefs was a clear conviction that God loved them as individuals. Their experience of a personal friendship with God was a new idea to Wesley and it was not one that he liked particularly. However, the voyage was marred by a series of violent storms and while he was terrified he observed that the Moravians had a calm confidence that God would save them. When Wesley eventually returned to England he introduced himself to Moravians in London and as a result he experienced, to his own surprise, a spiritual conversion. Of this he wrote:

> In the evening I went very unwillingly to a society in Aldersgate Street where one was reading Luther's preface to the Epistle to the Romans. About a quarter before nine, while he was describing the change which God works in the heart through faith in Christ, I felt my heart strangely warmed. I felt I did trust in Christ, Christ alone for salvation; and an assurance was given me that He had taken away my sins, even mine, and saved me from the law of sin and death.

It can be seen from this quotation that at the centre of Methodism is the experience of a strong relationship with God.

It was never the intention of John Wesley to set up a rival

organisation to the Church of England, but he felt that he had to try to reach those people who never set foot inside a church. To do this he set up groups which met in one another's houses. In addition Methodist ministers started preaching in the open air because many priests in the Church of England refused to let them use their pulpits. The man who started this was George Whitefield who preached to the miners of Kingswood, near Bristol. Yet Wesley never intended that this should be a substitute for meeting in a church. In early Methodism there were both travelling preachers and local preachers attached to a church. At first Wesley tried to keep the rules of the Church of England by allowing only ordained priests to preach. But eventually he allowed anyone to preach if they felt that God wanted them to do this, and now there are a great many 'lay preachers' in the Methodist Church who are not ordained ministers.

John Wesley is famous for saying that 'the world is my parish' and he proved this by travelling on horseback to preach throughout the British Isles. The usual means of travel in those days was by stagecoach but this was expensive and the early Methodists had to walk or travel by horse. In 50 years of preaching Wesley travelled about a quarter of a million miles.

It was only after the Methodist movement was about 50 years old that it finally broke with the Church of England. Wesley gave it separate legal status in 1784 with the *Deed of Declaration*. Separation from the Church of England came when Wesley became aware of the urgent need to send ministers to America, for very few had stayed there after the American War of Independence in 1776. The Bishop of London thought that it was enough to send three ministers to America. In 1784 Wesley ordained two men as preachers to go to America, and then three more. The Methodist Church spread throughout North America, the West Indies, Sri Lanka, India, China and Africa. There are now 19 million Methodists in the world with 13 million in the United States and 650,000 in Britain.

Methodism has always had a strong tradition of hymn singing. It is in these hymns that you will find the distinctive ideas and beliefs of Methodism. Charles Wesley wrote 5500 hymns to express his religious beliefs. The distinctive beliefs of Methodism are, first, that it is possible to experience a strong personal relationship with God and Jesus Christ, and, second, that it is vitally important for both ministers

Sometimes children accompany their parents to the Communion Rail and are given a blessing by the minister while their parents and other Church members receive communion.

and lay people to show their commitment to Christianity by actively helping others as Christ himself did. In view of this it is worth looking at John Wesley's personal motto:

    Do all the good you can,
    By all the means you can,
    In all the ways you can,
    In all the places you can,
    At all the times you can,
    To all the people you can,
    As long as ever you can.

Methodist Churches are very simple and bare. They usually have rows of pews with a gallery for the choir and organ. At the front is a wooden table with a cross on it and behind it there is a large pulpit which dominates the building and emphasises the importance of the spoken word. It is the intention that no ornamentation should distract the congregation from the word of God. At communion, which is not such a frequent service in Methodism as in the Church of England, the congregation sometimes stay in their places and small individual glasses of wine or grape juice and small pieces of bread are brought to those taking communion. This practice has become less common in recent years as the Methodists and the Church of England draw closer together.

The principal Methodist service, like that of other Nonconformist Churches, is the worship of God by means of hymns, prayers and the preaching of the minister. In some countries bishops hold the highest office in the Methodist Church, but there are no Methodist bishops in Britain. Methodist ministers are helped by lay readers; these are people who have had some theological training and who are allowed to preach and hold services in Methodist churches.

Unlike the Roman Catholic Church and the Church of England, the Methodist Church now ordains women as ministers, as well as Deaconesses in the 'Wesley Deaconess Order'.

The Methodist Church began its life as a breakaway movement from the Church of England and after that it broke into even smaller groups such as Independent Methodists, Primitive Methodists, and so on. Most of these smaller groups have since reunited and, most important of all, there has been an attempt to reunite the Methodist Church with the Anglican Church. A scheme was devised for this unification and Methodists and Anglicans voted on it in 1969. A 75 per cent majority was needed for it to succeed. 77 per cent of Methodists voted for it, but only 69 per cent of Anglicans. A second vote was held in 1972 but with no more success, even though the voting was close. The majority of both Churches would like to see only one Church, but there are still quite a number of Anglicans and some Methodists who are unhappy about it. It is likely, however, that in the near future the Methodist Church in England will lose its separate identity by becoming one with the Church of England, for even now Methodists and Anglicans can share their churches and their services.

1 How did the Methodist movement begin?
2 What important new contribution did John and Charles Wesley make to Christianity in England?
3 Try to visit a Methodist church. What differences are there between its design and that of other churches you have seen?
4 What would be the advantages, or disadvantages, in your view, of the Methodist Church becoming one with the Church of England?

7

The Nonconformist Churches

When Queen Elizabeth I made sure that the Church of England would keep to a middle path between the Roman Catholic Church and the Lutheran Church, there were some groups of people who were disappointed that the Reformation in England had not gone far enough and they refused to *conform* to the religion of the Church of England. It was these groups of people who, early in the seventeenth century, founded the first of the Nonconformist Churches. The main reason for the setting up of these Churches was that the Nonconformists disliked the way in which the priests of the Church of England controlled the sacraments and church services, and dominated the Christian life of the country. They believed that Jesus Christ is the only Head of the Church and that everyone else is equal under him. They refused to have priests in their Church and instead had 'elders' or 'presbyters'. So the first of these Nonconformist Churches was called the *Presbyterian Church*. There are now 50 million Presbyterians, but only in Scotland does this Church predominate. The Presbyterian Church there is known as the *Church of Scotland*.

The *Congregational Church* is very similar. Congregationalists practise democracy in the Church: every congregation is independent with no bishop in authority, but with a minister as the leader of the congregation. They celebrate their church services in a very simple way, concentrating on the singing of hymns, reading the Bible, and the preaching of the minister, who often makes up his own prayers to express the needs of the congregation. Because the Presbyterian Church of England and the Congregational Church of England are so similar, they decided in 1972 to unite in a single Church which is now known as the *United Reformed Church*.

All Churches baptise with water a person who wants to become a member of the Christian Church. Baptism, however, is not just like

Occasionally baptisms are performed in the sea (in this case because of drought in the summer of 1976) by immersion under the waves.

taking out a membership card for the Church; it is a sign of the person's faith that God has freed him from sin and evil, and will continue his life after death. For about 300 years the early Church only baptised adults or young people who knew what they were doing in asking to be baptised. That is to say, the Church did not baptise babies because they were too young to know what was being done to them. Not only that but a person was baptised, not by having water sprinkled or poured over his head, but by being pushed right under the water in a pool or in a stream. Being pushed under the water was a symbol of dying with Christ, and emerging from the water was a symbol of rising with Christ from the dead. By about the fourth century it became common for Christian parents to have their children baptised just after they were born, mainly because a large proportion of babies at that time and even until this century died in infancy. These early Christians believed that no one could be saved outside the Church and they baptised their children so that all the family could be with God when they died.

At the time of the Reformation, however, there were groups of Protestants who insisted on going back to the old practice of only baptising those who believed in Christianity, and never baptising children. These people were known as *Anabaptists*. This comes from the Greek and means 'to baptise again'. The Anabaptists ignored infant baptism and baptised people only when they were old enough to understand what it meant, and the original Anabaptists baptised themselves again to make up for what they believed were the deficiencies of their childhood baptism. One of these men was *John Smyth*, who went to Amsterdam in exile from England in 1609. He went there because he would not conform with Queen Elizabeth's Church of England. It was Smyth and other exiles from England who formed the first *Baptist Church* of England, but it was formed on the continent. In 1612 the first Baptist congregation was set up in London when Thomas Helwys came back from Holland. Baptist churches, like other Nonconformist churches, are dominated by a large pulpit at the far end of the church. But at the foot of the pulpit in a Baptist church you will find a pool with tiles and steps going down into it. There are taps to fill it with water, and the minister and the person being baptised go down into the water where the baptised person is immersed under the water. In place of infant baptism Baptists now have a service of *dedication* to God for their children.

There are about 30 million baptised members of the Baptist Church but there may be three times as many people associated with the Church. Twenty-six million of these are in the United States and many are negroes. Surprisingly perhaps, there is a very vigorous Baptist Church in the Soviet Union, though the Baptists there are not approved of by the government and have been persecuted recently by the police. Some Russian Baptists have even been sent to prison camps. American Baptists include the evangelist Billy Graham and the late Martin Luther King (see p. 70) but the most famous English Baptist was John Bunyan who wrote *The Pilgrim's Progress*, a long parable on the Christian life, when he was in Bedford prison for his religious views in 1678.

The *Society of Friends*, usually known as the *Quakers*, is the most

John Bunyan (1628–1688)

individual of the Nonconformist Churches. They have no creed and no ministers, nor do they believe in having consecrated or special buildings. They come together in Meeting Houses which are simply-furnished rooms. Here they sit in silence which is broken only when someone in the group feels that he has something to say. Quaker 'Meetings for Worship' are thus quite unprogrammed and spontaneous. The Quaker movement was founded in the middle of the seventeenth century by George Fox, and they got their name because Fox told Judge Bennett in 1650 to tremble and quake at the Word of God. Quakers are best known because of their social work. They include Elizabeth Fry, who helped to reform the prisons of Britain in the early nineteenth century, and the chocolate manufacturing families of Rowntree and Cadbury. Joseph Rowntree, who died in 1925, was famous for making sure that his workers were well paid and worked in good conditions, and he built houses and schools for them. Since his time the Rowntree Trust has been set up which donates money mainly for use in race relations work. Most Quakers are pacifists, which means that they refuse to fight and kill under any circumstances and so they always refuse to join any army.

In the past they have suffered because of this, preferring to go to prison rather than be conscripted into the army, but this does not often happen now.

The last of the Nonconformist Churches is the Methodist Church which broke away from the Church of England in 1784, but this has already been described in some detail. These Churches are often known as the Free Churches because, unlike the Church of England, they are free from control by the monarch and by the government.

At the beginning of the twentieth century a number of *Pentecostal Churches* were founded mainly in North America, and so they are not strictly 'Nonconformist' Churches. The members of these Churches look for a baptism in the Holy Spirit and for direct experiences of the Holy Spirit including 'speaking with tongues' which is mentioned in the New Testament. They want to relive the original Pentecost described in *Acts*, Ch. 2. In more recent years this wish to experience the Spirit has spread to many other Churches throughout the world and has become known as the *charismatic movement*. It is sometimes associated with faith healing, the healing of a sick person through belief that God will heal them. The charismatic movement has often been popular with young people and has resulted in various groups such as the *Jesus Freaks* and the *Jesus Movement*. The charismatic movement is a sign of how many people feel the need to rediscover Christianity as an immediate and living experience, though it is a movement that does not suit everyone.

1 Why are the 'Nonconformist' Churches so called?
2 The Nonconformist Churches broke away in order to preserve what they considered was an important part of Christianity which was being ignored by the larger Churches. Read *John*, Ch. 17, vv. 20–23 for one view on the unity of the Church.
3 Do you think young children should be baptised? It is becoming less common for parents to baptise their children automatically. Would you baptise your children?
4 Read *Pilgrim's Progress*. You could try listening to part of the opera of the same name by Ralph Vaughan Williams. (It is recorded on SLS 959.)
5 How did the Presbyterian Church get its name?
6 Find out what you can about Elizabeth Fry and her work in prison reform.
7 What is a 'pacifist'? Do you agree with pacifism? Give your reasons.
8 Find out more about the Jesus Movement. You can find some information in Ian Birnie's book *Christianity and Youth* (published by Edward Arnold).
9 Discover what you can about faith healing and exorcism, both of which are associated with the charismatic movement. What are they? Who practises them? Why do they do this? Do they do any good? Are there any drawbacks?
10 There are two films available from Concord Films on this area: *George Fox* (*From Inner Space*) (an ABC TV production, black and white, 30 mins, 1966) and *Cries From Within*, recent searches for the spiritual in the modern world (colour, 60 mins, 1973).

8

The World Council of Churches

In looking at the history of the Christian Church we have tended to emphasise the disunity of the Church because this has been the dominant fact about the last 400 years of the Church and because we have been looking at the different denominations of the Church. During the last 50 years, however, Christians have become more and more aware of the stupidity and uselessness of having so many Churches. The Roman Catholic Church, too, now recognises this, though Catholics still believe that their Church has preserved something of particular value over the centuries and this makes them somewhat hesitant about coming together with other Churches. In recent years there has been a strong movement towards the Churches co-operating and reuniting. This is usually called the *Ecumenical Movement*. A short time ago, as we have seen, two separate Churches united in Britain. The Congregational Church and the Presbyterian Church of England decided to merge in 1972 to form the United Reformed Church. Recently the Church of England and the Methodists voted on whether they should become one Church. The Methodists voted to accept this, but some Anglicans voted against it because of some of the conditions involved. However, it is likely that there will be another vote in the future and it may well be that they will decide to unite.

In 1948 an organisation was formed which tried to bring all the Churches together. This is the *World Council of Churches*. This is not an extra Church. It is the Churches' equivalent of the United Nations Organisation, where all the Churches who are members can come together to talk about their beliefs—what they have in common and what separates them—and about how they can agree to co-operate in practical projects to help other people. The World Council of Churches now has 271 member Churches. The only major Church

The symbol of the World Council of Churches is displayed at a work camp.

which has not yet joined is the Roman Catholic Church, but as it has already sent official 'observers', it may decide to join in the future. The Council has a full meeting every seven years and has previously met in Amsterdam, Evanston (Illinois), New Delhi, and Uppsala in Sweden. The most recent meeting was in Vancouver (Canada) in 1983. Dr Philip Potter, a Methodist minister from Trinidad, became secretary of the World Council of Churches in 1972.

Like the United Nations, but on a much smaller scale, the World Council of Churches finances educational and health projects throughout the world. One of the first things it did after the 1939–45 war was to look after and find homes for refugees and migrants. These people were not only homeless, but had often been forced to leave their own country as a result of the Nazis' use of slave labour. The World Council of Churches also promotes theological and religious education mainly in Europe and it tries to support even small discussion groups that take place in people's homes. In a number of oppressed countries, mainly in southern Africa, it has sent money for education and for medical supplies to organisations of freedom fighters who are trying to free their countries from political oppression. Although the money has been sent for education and medical supplies, this action has met with some opposition from those Christians who think that it is wrong to support, even indirectly, groups who use violence to achieve their aims. Much of this opposition has come from bishops in the Church of England. But increasingly over the last few years, especially since Philip Potter, a black West Indian, became secretary, the World Council of Churches has become more active in opposing racialism.

There is a similar organisation in Britain for bringing the various Churches together and this is the British Council of Churches.

Dr Philip Potter

Young people helping to build a youth centre in Greece, during a work camp organised by the World Council of Churches.

1 What is the Ecumenical Movement? What, do you think, can be done to further its aims?
2 Should the World Council of Churches contribute money and supplies to guerrilla fighters? Would you contribute to their funds?
3 *One Out Of Many*, a film on the work of the World Council of Churches, can be hired from Christian Aid, P.O. Box 1, London SW9 8BH.

9

The Church Abroad

When we think of Christianity we naturally tend to think of what it is like in Britain. Christianity, however, is not confined to Britain and it is not even confined to Europe and North America. Christianity is a worldwide religion, stronger in some countries than in others. This should not be surprising because it did not begin in Europe. Christianity started in Palestine when it was a small province of the Roman Empire. The first centre of Christianity was Jerusalem, which is in Asia. Christianity became the major religion of Europe only after the Emperor Constantine had been baptised in the fourth century. The inhabitants of Europe first became aware of how big the world is in the fifteenth century when Columbus discovered the American continent while he was trying to get to India. Soon afterwards Spanish and Portuguese explorers went to South America and took priests with them to convert the inhabitants to Christianity—as well as to exploit the wealth of those countries. No sooner had Marco Polo been to China than missionaries set off in the sixteenth century to convert the Chinese. The most famous of these missionaries to the East was *St Francis Xavier*, who did most of his work in Japan.

In the years after the Reformation in England a group of Puritans, who found it difficult to practise their religion in England, set off for North America in the *Mayflower*. In 1620 these 'Pilgrim Fathers' took Christianity to the United States. When Great Britain acquired colonies in the eighteenth and nineteenth centuries in the West Indies, Africa, India and Australia, the colonists took Christianity with them. This is how Christianity was spread throughout the world and many Protestant and Roman Catholic missionaries are still active in most countries of the world. Some have even been killed for this, as happened not so long ago in the Congo and Uganda.

What do missionaries do abroad? Their principal jobs are to run schools to educate the local children and to run hospitals and medical centres. They also train people so that they can take over the schools and hospitals for themselves. In recent years they have had to organise emergency aid in areas of famine; they also teach the local inhabitants advanced techniques of growing food. In addition to all this they teach people about Christ and Christianity, and they try to convert people by the example of their lives.

Perhaps the best-known of all twentieth-century missionaries was *Albert Schweitzer*. He was a very remarkable man but he was also a man of some contradictions. Schweitzer was born in 1875. He was a theologian and at the turn of the century wrote two very important books about the life of Jesus which are still read today. He was also a world famous organist and was the first to make the organ music of Bach well known. But then he decided to give up all this to train as a doctor so that he could become, at the age of 38, a missionary in Africa. He went to the small village of Lambarene where he built a hospital. He stayed there until he died in 1965 at the age of 90.

The Africans at Lambarene were devoted to Schweitzer, but he was criticised by Europeans because he detested modern inventions and not only refused to have cars in Lambarene but even refused to have electricity and running water in his hospital. He also thought that white people were naturally superior to Africans even though he devoted his life to them.

The current trend in missionary work is to start churches but eventually to leave and allow the local Christians to take over their own church.

What is the attitude of Christianity to other religions? As Christian missionaries have spread the message of Jesus Christ across the globe they have come into contact with non-Christian religions and sometimes they have come into conflict with them. In the past Christians have often fought with those who followed other religions but nowadays Christians respect these and share some of their beliefs, for example belief in God and the need to live a good life. Christians also believe that they can learn something from other religions. But Christianity is different from other religions and Christians believe that it is a better and truer religion, which is why missionaries have taken the message of Christ to other countries. Christians believe that God has sent Jesus Christ as his unique representative to free the human race and they believe that it is of the greatest importance that other people should know this.

Unfortunately, different Churches have often competed with each other in making converts to Christianity. This is obviously very stupid and very wasteful where there are only a few missionaries covering a large area. It was happening, for example, in South India, but the result was that all the Protestant Churches there united in the Church of South India. This was formed in 1947 so that Protestant Christians could co-operate in their work there.

1 What is a 'missionary'? Find out the origin of the word.
2 People often say that they have a 'vocation' to be a missionary or a priest. Discover the meaning of the word 'vocation'.
3 Do you think it matters which religion a person belongs to? Do you think that Christians have a right to convert others?
4 Egypt and some other countries do not allow Christian missionaries to work there. Why do you think they do this? Do you agree with them?
5 If it is possible, ask your teacher to invite someone who has worked as a missionary to talk to the class. Ask them about their work.
6 A film can be hired from Concord Films called *Christ and Disorder*. It is a survey of the Church throughout the world in the light of the Ecumenical Movement (BBC, black and white, 50 mins, 1968)

The teaching of agricultural techniques is now part of missionary work.

10

What Christians Do

So far we have emphasised that Christians belong to certain Churches and that they hold certain beliefs. But being a Christian is also a way of life. This means that Christians live their life in a special kind of way. They do certain things because they are Christian and what they do is based on the example of Jesus Christ. How Christians behave towards other people can be summed up in the words of Jesus, 'Love your neighbour as yourself,' and 'Do to others as you would want them to do to you.'

St Paul wrote a famous passage in *1 Corinthians*, Ch. 13 in which he says that whatever possessions and natural talents we may have, life is worthless unless we have love for other people. Love, he says, has a number of qualities. Love shows patience and kindness; a person with love is not jealous, arrogant or rude; he does not insist on his own way; he is not irritable and he puts up with things he does not like. Christianity, then, is not a religion which is based on revenge, personal honour or self-interest, as are the lives of many people, but it is a religion of love. Yet love is not just a feeling or emotion, it is a reason for doing things for other people. The first Christians shared all their possessions and money; they kept as much as they needed and gave away the rest to the poor. Similarly, in the Middle Ages it was the monks who had the responsibility for educating people. Monasteries were places where the poor could go for a meal. But what do Christians do in the world today?

Monks and nuns are still involved in helping people as they have been for centuries. Much of this is done outside Europe by missionaries who run schools and hospitals. Perhaps the best known is a Catholic nun in India, *Mother Theresa*. She works with a group of nuns in Calcutta. Calcutta is a city of eight million people where the poor congregate from villages in the hope of finding work. But there

is no work for all these people and there is not enough food. Each night some of them die on the streets from cold and starvation. In such an enormous city Mother Theresa and her helpers can do only a little but they house and feed as many people as they can. The work they do is a sign of God's love through which they try to keep alive the hope that life is still worth living.

There are, of course, many thousands of people like Mother Theresa who will never become famous. One person whose work is still remembered is *Martin Luther King*. He was a negro and a Baptist minister. Before he was murdered in 1968 he was the leader of a movement of black Americans who were attempting to free themselves from the prejudice of white Americans. Under Luther King, the Civil Rights Movement, as it was called, succeeded in changing many of the laws of the United States which made life unjust for black Americans. It became illegal to exclude blacks from

schools and universities, restaurants, trains, buses and places of employment. Martin Luther King was arrested by the police during a demonstration in 1963, but he was awarded the Nobel Peace Prize in the following year for his work on civil rights. Luther King was one of many Christians who are struggling to free their fellow men from injustice and oppression.

Being a Christian involves committing yourself to other people. Apart from the many individuals who do this there is one Christian group which was formed specifically to help others. When General William Booth founded the *Salvation Army* in 1865 there were enormous social problems in the U.K. but there were no social workers to help solve them. The Salvation Army is organised on military lines but their fight is against poverty and lack of Christian belief, that is, against what they see as material and spiritual poverty. They are best known for singing hymns and for their brass bands, but most of their time and energy goes into running over 200 homes of various kinds in Britain. They run homes and hostels for tramps, ex-criminals, unmarried mothers, handicapped children and old people.

What Christians Do 71

It is by serving those in need in this way that the Salvation Army hopes that people will come to know God. They are active in 83 countries throughout the world and are particularly strong in the United States where they also run hospitals and schools.

Organisations which raise money to help others are known as 'charities'. There are many charities which are not Christian organisations but which were started by Christians. Christians were among those who started OXFAM (the Oxford Committee for Famine Relief) in 1942. Similarly the *Samaritans* were started by an Anglican priest, the Rev. Chad Varah. The Samaritans is an organisation which gives advice over the telephone to those who are desperate and suicidal. It is not a Christian organisation; anyone can become a Samaritan and anyone can ask for help without expecting a parson on the end of the phone. But it was the story of the Good Samaritan in Luke's Gospel that inspired Chad Varah to start this work. Many orphanages like Dr Barnardo's Homes, the Cheshire

Homes and almost all homes for unmarried mothers are run by Christian groups.

There is one other special organisation which should be mentioned. We read earlier that the British Council of Churches is a group of all the Churches which are to be found in Britain (apart from the Roman Catholic Church). As you would expect, the Churches felt that they ought to play their part in helping the poor and underfed in other parts of the world. *Christian Aid* was founded by the British Council of Churches to do this. Christian Aid raises money and organises helpers for practical projects. It raises over £3 million a year, mainly during Christian Aid week. This money is spent on emergencies such as famines, floods and earthquakes, and on development projects which help people to grow their own food by providing tractors, seed, fertilisers and so on. Christian Aid co-operates with the work being done by the World Council of Churches and Catholic groups like the Catholic Fund for Overseas Development (CAFOD). It also tries to educate people and to inform them about the problems that exist in the world, the reasons why they exist and how they might be solved. All this requires much time, energy and money. But being a Christian involves serving other people and following the example of Jesus Christ. As the Apostle James said, 'Religion that is pure and undefiled before God the Father is this, to visit orphans and widows in their distress.'

1 There are many passages in the New Testament which form the basis for the way Christians should behave. Here are some of them; look them up. *Matthew*, Ch. 11, vv. 2–6; Ch. 22, vv. 34–40; Ch. 25, vv. 31–46; *Luke*, Ch. 10, vv. 29–37; 1 *Corinthians*, Ch. 13; *James*, Ch. 1, vv. 22–27. List the qualities and types of action that are required of a Christian in these passages. Now think of present-day conditions and list what action should be expected of a Christian today.
2 Can you think of any group of people in Britain that needs help and is not getting it? What could be done to help them, especially in your own town?
3 Find out what you can about Martin Luther King, Albert Schweitzer and Mother Theresa. There is a section on Luther King

in Ian Birnie's book *Four Working for Humanity*. A book on Mother Theresa by Sheila M. Hobden is available in Birnie's series *People With A Purpose*.
4 Organising help is a *very* complex business. Imagine that you work for Christian Aid and that you have to lead a team of workers to help feed people suffering from famine and drought in Africa at the southern edge of the Sahara desert. How will you plan your work and organise your team? Who will you take with you and what would you take? Think of everything that will have to be done.
5 A list of films and slides showing the work of Christian Aid can be obtained by writing to or telephoning Christian Aid, P.O. Box 1, London SW9 8BH (phone 01 733 5500).

The following films can be hired from Concord Films: '*I Have a Dream . . .*' *The Life of Martin Luther King* (black and white, 30 mins, 1971); *Mother Theresa of Calcutta* (black and white, 15 mins, 1964); *Where the People Are* (black and white, 30 mins, 1969) which deals with a young minister from a conventional background who comes to question the Vietnam war and war in general.

Films can also be hired from BBC Education and Training, Film and Video Hire Library, The Guild Organization, Guild House, Oundle Road, Peterborough PE2 9PZ (who also supply a catalogue).

11

How Christians Worship

Worship is the act of coming together to pray and to praise God. There are two forms of prayer, private and public, and it is usual for Christians to perform both. Prayer is simply talking to God and Christians do this because they believe that God cares for them and that he can help them. It is not, however, only Christians who pray and worship. This is an indispensable part of all other religions. Some people find private prayer more suitable than going to church services, while others find private prayer difficult and prefer to go to church with others. In private prayer people talk to God as they would to a friend. In prayer it is possible to find a calmness which is not possible while people rush about in their jobs and in their life at home. Prayer does not always involve asking for something, it just involves talking and thinking.

Public prayer consists of a group of people gathering together to say prayers that they want to share (people often pray for each other), to sing hymns or to read the Bible together. They sometimes meet for the sacraments: to baptise someone, for a marriage, or to share the eucharist, the meal of bread and wine. It is on these public occasions that people see, in part, what the Church is like. The way in which worship takes place varies from Church to Church and from country to country. In Britain a Roman Catholic service is very different from, say, a Methodist service. But there would also be some differences between what Roman Catholics do in Britain and what they do in Italy or Japan. Each person has his own preference but most people prefer the type of service they were introduced to as children. To give a rough idea of how different these services can be, if you went to a Catholic church on a Sunday morning you would find yourself at mass (i.e. the eucharist). If you went into a Church of England church you might be at the eucharist though you would probably be at Matins which includes the singing of hymns and psalms, readings from the Bible, prayers and a sermon; and similar services are held in other Protestant churches. But if you went to a meeting of the Society of Friends (the Quakers) most of the time would be spent in silence.

Worship usually takes place in churches, in special buildings, although you sometimes find small groups of Christians who meet in a house. Even the churches of different denominations look different. The most impressive of these buildings are cathedrals, most of which were built in the Middle Ages. The finest of these medieval cathedrals are to be found in France, but the best of the English medieval cathedrals can be seen at Durham, York, Gloucester, Wells, Ely and Canterbury. There are some modern cathedrals, too, such as the Catholic cathedral in Liverpool and the Anglican cathedral at Coventry which was opened and consecrated in 1962, the old cathedral having been destroyed in the last war. These buildings often contain religious works of art like paintings, sculptures and stained glass. Coventry cathedral, for example, contains among other things a large tapestry of Christ raised from the dead by Graham Sutherland. The Catholic cathedral in Liverpool, however, cost the people of Liverpool £4 million and it is likely that in the future the money that

Coventry Cathedral

the Church raises will be spent on people rather than on buildings. And as the number of active Christians is decreasing in Britain at the moment, it is less likely that they will be able to or will want to build showpieces like the cathedrals of Liverpool and Coventry. This was possible in the Middle Ages when the populations of towns like Canterbury and Chartres could spend over 100 years building a huge cathedral which was a symbol of their belief and which was itself an act of worship. But conditions have changed and it is not possible today.

Christians regard their whole life as an act of worship if they live as they think God would want them to live. There are some groups of people, however, who devote a large part of their daily life to worshipping God in a formal way. These are the communities of monks and nuns who spend several hours every day in prayer. Three or four times a day they will come together to chant psalms, to pray and to go to mass. Religious communities are not a thing of the past; there are several hundred in Britain today.

The Church keeps a large number of festivals throughout the year, and they are repeated year after year. The Church year begins at the end of November with *Advent* which is a penitential season of four weeks which prepares the way for Christmas. *Christmas* (originally Christ-mass) is always kept on 25 December and celebrates the birth of Jesus. *Boxing Day* is the feast of St Stephen, the first Christian martyr, who was killed by a group of Jews which included Saul who later became St Paul. *Epiphany* is on 6 January and recalls the story of the wise men offering their gifts. There are many other festivals for saints, but the next big date is *Ash Wednesday* (preceded by Shrove Tuesday) when *Lent* begins. This is the second penitential season and it lasts for 40 days during which Jesus's 40 days in the desert are remembered. Then *Palm Sunday*, *Maundy Thursday* (the day of the Last Supper and the betrayal of Jesus), *Good Friday* and *Easter Sunday* all follow in rapid succession. For a Christian, Easter Sunday is the most important day of the year, for this is when he will celebrate the raising up of Jesus after his death. The other important festival is *Pentecost* (Whitsunday), when the Church recalls the coming of the Holy Spirit to the Apostles. All these different festivals are remembered in church services by different Bible readings, different prayers and different symbolic actions.

How Christians Worship 77

1 Compile a list of the major Church festivals, giving the date for the present year.
2 Where are the prayers of the Church of England to be found?
3 Find out what a 'missal' is.
4 If you went to a service would you prefer a formal service in a church or a less formal and more intimate service in someone's house?
5 If you went to a church service what kind of service would you like and what would you prefer to avoid? For example, do you like or dislike ritual, the singing of hymns, etc?
6 Assemblies in most schools are still acts of worship. Do you think this is a good thing?
7 Music has always been used in worship from the earliest chants to modern pop music. Listen to some different examples if you can. Do you think that *Jesus Christ Superstar* and *Godspell* are acts of worship?
8 Try to visit a cathedral.
9 A wide range of slides of English and French cathedrals is available from The Slide Centre, 143 Chatham Road, London SW11 6SR.

A scene from the film of Jesus Christ Superstar

12

The Future of Christianity

Throughout this survey of modern Christianity we have been looking at Churches. The importance of Christianity, however, cannot be summed up just by looking at these organisations and institutions. If a person decides to be a Christian it is because of what he thinks about God, about himself and about other people, and it is because of how he decides to live his life. A person becomes a Christian as a result of his own personal *experience*. In fact there are a lot of people who say that they are Christians—they accept Christian beliefs and try to live a good life—but they find it difficult to be in a Church. They often find church services unattractive. So it is possible to be a Christian without going to church. But if someone is a religious person, if their experience has made them want to be a Christian, they will want to share this experience with others. They will want to talk to others who have had a similar experience of life. And this is why Christians join these organisations and go to church.

Christianity is the biggest religion in the world; it has about 1000 million members. Yet it is obvious that Christianity has suffered a serious decline in numbers recently in Europe and particularly in Britain. Thirty years ago it could be said that England was a Christian country but this is no longer possible. It is, however, worth bearing in mind that Scotland, Wales and Ireland have a stronger religious tradition than England has. Only a minority of people in Britain are practising Christians, though there are still several million people who are. As a result of this trend people have started to ask whether Christianity will survive at all. One result of this reduction in numbers is that as each Church has become smaller, all the Churches have moved closer together. It is hoped by many that eventually all the Churches will unite as one Church.

A group of friends celebrate the eucharist at home.

But is this enough? Even if all these separate Churches unite, can the Christian Church still survive? And if it survives, what will the Church look like in the future? Christians certainly believe that God will preserve his Church but it is likely that there will be many changes in the Church of the future. As there are now fewer committed Christians in Britain, we are going to see fewer church buildings. Christians are likely to form small local groups which meet in each other's houses or in community centres for services and discussions. Clergymen may find that they no longer have a full-time job and they may take a part-time job as well, such as teaching. Think of all the churches in your town and all the clergymen who run them. Do we need all these buildings and all these full-time priests and ministers? One difficulty is that clergymen often try to do too much organising; they would find it easier if they shared this work with lay people, and if lay people accepted their responsibilities.

This movement towards small local groups of Christians has already started in a number of places. One such place is an estate in Corby New Town, Northamptonshire. If you go to the estate and look for a church with a spire and stained glass windows and a churchyard, you will not find one. But there is a small and very active group of Christians on the estate. Each Sunday they meet in a special hall called the Worship Room in the Communicare Centre. This hall is also used for dances, drinking, youth clubs, playgroups, and so on. There is also a small chapel which is always open for quiet and private prayer. There are two ministers for the estate: a Church of England priest and a Baptist minister who represents the Nonconformist Churches. All these Protestant Christians share the same Sunday services. The Christians on this estate do not see themselves as a group which is separate from everyone else. They are people who have a contribution to make to the local community.

In the future we may find that the Church begins to look more like the Church of the first century after the death of Jesus. In those days Christianity was made up of many small groups scattered throughout the towns of the Roman Empire, all preaching the good news about Jesus. That is how it all began and is how Christianity may develop in the years to come.

1. While Christianity is expanding in some parts of the world, do you think that it will survive in Britain? If not, explain why not. If it survives, how will it have to change?
2. Many jobs traditionally done by the Church (the running of schools, hospitals, etc.) are now done by the government and local authorities. What jobs can still be done by the Church?
3. What could be done in your town to change and improve the Christian Church?
4. *Beggar At The Gate*, a film available from Concord Films, asks whether the Church will shift from its concern with traditional ritual towards an involvement with the problems of the world (colour, 56 mins).

© Geoffrey Turner 1977

First published in Great Britain 1977 by
Edward Arnold (Publishers) Ltd
41 Bedford Square   London WC1B 3DQ

Reprinted 1979, 1984

British Library Cataloguing in Publication Data
Turner, Geoffrey
  Christianity.
  1. Christianity
  I. Title
  202'.4'372   BR121.2
ISBN 0-7131-0144-X

Edward Arnold (Australia) Pty Ltd
80 Waverley Road, Caulfield East
Victoria 3145, Australia

All Rights Reserved. No part of this publication may be reproduced, stored in a retrieval system, or transmitted in any form or by any means, electronic, mechanical, photocopying, recording or otherwise, without the prior permission of Edward Arnold (Publishers) Ltd.

Printed in Great Britain by
The Camelot Press Ltd, Southampton